D1296350

THE
HAIKU
ANTHOLOGY

THE
HAIKU
ANTHOLOGY

ENGLISH LANGUAGE HAIKU BY
CONTEMPORARY AMERICAN
AND CANADIAN POETS

Edited with an Introduction by
Cor van den Heuvel

1974
Anchor Books
Anchor Press/Doubleday
Garden City, New York

Acknowledgments

The editor thanks the following poets, magazines, and publishers
for permission to print these poems (AH: *American Haiku;* HM:
Haiku Magazine; HW: *Haiku West;* HH: *Haiku Highlights;* MH:
Modern Haiku):

Mary Acosta: "dark summer lake" from MH, Vol. II, No. 3, copy-
right © 1971 by Kay Titus Mormino; by permission of the author.

Eric Amann: "Billboards" from HM, Vol. 1, No. 1 (1967); "Snow
falling" from *Haiku Spotlight* (Japan) #67, Jan. 3, 1970; "The
circus tent" from *Haiku Spotlight* #22, Feb. 22, 1969; by per-
mission of the author.

Jack Cain: "an empty elevator" and "waiting" from HM, Vol. 3,
No. 4, copyright 1969 by Eric W. Amann; "someone's newspaper"
and "empty room" from HM, Vol. 3, No. 2, copyright 1969 by
Eric W. Amann; by permission of the author.

l.a. davidson: "beyond" from HM, Vol. 5, No. 3, © William J.
Higginson 1972; by permission of the author.

Frances Drivas: "morning" from HM, Vol. 5, No. 3, © William J.
Higginson 1972; by permission of the author.

and "beyond the porch" to be published by HM, courtesy of William J. Higginson, editor; by permission of the author.

Kenneth Yasuda: "Summer Trees," "Crimson Dragonfly—I," and "Crimson Dragonfly—II" from *The Japanese Haiku*, published by Charles E. Tuttle Company, Inc., Rutland, Vermont, and Tokyo, Japan, © 1957 by Charles E. Tuttle Co., Inc.; by permission of the publisher and the author.

Virginia Brady Young: "During a downpour" from MH, Vol. III, No. 3, copyright © 1972 by Kay Titus Mormino; "Ridges of snow," "On the first day of spring," "In a circle of thaw," "fallen birch leaf," and "The silence" from *Circle of Thaw*, published by Barlenmir House, New York, New York, copyright © 1972 by Virginia Brady Young; by permission of the author.

TO HAROLD G. HENDERSON AND R. H. BLYTH

The editor would like to thank the poets for their cooperation in putting together this book, particularly William J. Higginson for the benefit of his discerning criticism and the use of his extensive haiku library, and Anita Virgil for suggestions and insights that were—though we did not always agree—an invaluable aid to making some of the more difficult editorial decisions. I would also like to express my appreciation to William Strachan, editor of Anchor Books, for his confidence in the original concept of this anthology and for his understanding and patience in helping make it a reality.

And, for her advice and encouragement, a special thank you to Leonia Larrecq—with love to "First Chrysanthemum."

CONTENTS[1]

[1] The haiku are identified by first lines—except for those by Kenneth Yasuda, which have titles. In some cases where the haiku comprise, or have been excerpted from, a longer work—such as a sequence—the title of that work is also given.

A NOTE ON THE SELECTION &
LAYOUT OF THE POEMS

Selection: Some readers may wonder why I've chosen
certain poems in this book which are, on the surface,
similar to others. If a haiku is a good one, it doesn't mat-
ter if the subject has been used before. The writing of
variations on certain subjects in haiku, sometimes using
the same or similar phrases (or even changing a few
words of a previous haiku), is one of the most interesting
challenges it offers a poet, and can result in refreshingly
different ways of "seeing anew" for the reader. This is
an aspect of traditional Japanese haiku which is hard for
many Westerners, with their ideas of uniqueness and
Romantic individualism, to accept. But some of the most
original voices in haiku do not hesitate to dare seeming
derivative if they see a way of reworking an "old" image.
Much experimentation is going on now that expands the
potential inherent in the haiku: the extension of form by
grouping haiku in sequences, or in variations, combin-
ing them with prose (*haibun*), or with other types of
poetry, as well as innovations in the form and content of
the single haiku. A number of haiku in this book—John
Wills's from *river*, for example—have been selected from
sequences and might have more depth in their original
context. (Some of these are indicated on the Contents
pages.) Two complete short sequences by Mabelsson
Norway and William J. Higginson are included.

Layout: Due to the fact that the words of a haiku provide only the bare essentials of the image, with which the reader's awareness works to create the haiku moment, it is important that the reader is not distracted from those essentials. The layout of the page, the amount of white space within which the words may work, and the choice of the other haiku on the spread all play a role in determining how the reader will direct his attention. Such considerations have been second only to the selection of the haiku themselves in the editing of this book.

INTRODUCTION

Until now, the poets represented in this anthology have been largely "invisible." Though some of them have been writing haiku for nearly two decades or longer, their work has flowered practically unnoticed—their only recognition coming from the small world of the haiku magazines. The movement of which they are a part, however, has now reached a point where its accomplishments can no longer be ignored.

Haiku in English got its real start in the fifties, when an avid interest in Japanese culture and religion swept the postwar United States.[1] Growing out of the increased contacts with Japan through the Occupation and a spiritual thirst for religious and artistic fulfillment, this interest centered on art, literature, and Zen Buddhism. Alan Watts, Donald Keene, D. T. Suzuki, the Beats, and others all contributed to both arousing and feeding this interest, but it was R. H. Blyth's extraordinary four-volume work *Haiku* (published between 1949 and 1952), Kenneth Yasuda's *The Japanese Haiku* (1957), and Harold G. Henderson's *An Introduction to Haiku*

[1] The Imagists, and those who followed them, had no real understanding of haiku. Because they had no adequate translations or critical analyses available, they failed to see the spiritual depth haiku embodies, or the unity of man and nature it reveals. English language haiku owes practically nothing to their experiments except in the sense that all modern poetry owes them a debt for their call for concision and clarity in language.

(1958) that provided for the first time the solid foundation necessary for the creation of haiku in English.[2]

In the late fifties and early sixties the seed began to germinate, and a few poets across the country began to write haiku with an awareness and understanding of its possibilities.

Within five years after the publication of Henderson's book, a magazine was started by James Bull in Platteville, Wisconsin, devoted solely to English language haiku: *American Haiku* (1963). The first issue was dedicated to Henderson and included a letter from him to the editors, which said in part: "If there is to be a real 'American Haiku' we must—by trial and error—work out our own standards. . . . One of the great functions *American Haiku* could perform is that of being a forum for the expression of divergent opinions." J. W. Hackett, Nicholas Virgilio, Mabelsson Norway (O Southard), and Larry Gates were among the contributors to that first issue.[3] The magazine was published twelve times in the next five years, ceasing publication in May 1968. Later the same year, under the auspices of the Japan Society, the Haiku Society of America was founded to promote the writing and appreciation of haiku.

In the meantime, three new haiku magazines had emerged, all of which are still publishing. Jean Calkins started *Haiku Highlights and Other Small Poems* (now called *Dragonfly: A Quarterly of Haiku Highlights*) in Kanona, New York, in 1965. Though the work it pub-

[2] Henderson published a small book on Japanese haiku, *The Bamboo Broom*, in 1934, in which he recognized the possibility of English haiku. But the time was not ripe. (There were exceptions: Clement Hoyt began studying Zen in 1936 with Nyogen Senzaki, the man who "taught me the haiku," and Yasuda was writing haiku in English in the thirties, publishing some as "Experiments in English" in *A Pepper Pod*, 1947.)

[3] Among those appearing in the second issue were Robert Spiess, Virginia Brady Young, Clement Hoyt, and Elizabeth Searle Lamb.

lished was undistinguished for a long time, in recent years it has printed significant articles on haiku by William J. Higginson, Michael McClintock, and others. In 1967 two haiku magazines appeared that were to carry on the work begun by *American Haiku: Haiku West,* edited by Leroy Kanterman in New York City, and *Haiku,* edited by Eric Amann in Toronto, Canada. (*Haiku* is now edited by William J. Higginson in Paterson, New Jersey.) Both have printed high quality haiku, and *Haiku* has especially demonstrated a willingness to experiment with haiku form and presentation.

There are now at least five English language haiku magazines being published in the United States, with others in England and Australia. In fact, haiku are being written all over the world—in German, French, Spanish, Portuguese, Italian, and other languages, as well as English and, of course, Japanese.[4]

In the midst of this proliferating interest and activity with haiku throughout the world, the "literary world"—critics and poets alike—sees English language haiku either as worthless fragments, blank and incomprehensible, or as little more than examples of a form of light verse whose only use is as an educational aid to interest children in poetry.[5] Such attitudes may have been ex-

[4] See Gary Brower's annotated bibliography, *Haiku in Western Languages* (1972).

[5] There are exceptions. A few well-known poets have tried to write haiku, but none has seen it as a principal "way" or direction for their work. Gary Snyder, though he was one of the first to try writing haiku in English with an understanding of Japanese haiku (as early as 1952), has never concentrated his poetic energies in that direction. Jack Kerouac, the Beat novelist, was also an early practitioner of haiku, and probably came closer than any of the Beat poets to its essence. But it remained a footnote to his other work. More recently, Hayden Carruth, Robert Kelly, John Hollander, and some other recognized poets have experimented with short poems which derive from the form of haiku, but show little or no conception of the haiku's true nature.

cused in the early years—thousands of bad poems were published under the name of haiku—but in the last few years the proportion of good haiku to bad has been at least the same as in any other kind of poetry.

One can only conclude that such critics have not looked deeply enough into the literature available on the Japanese haiku and its esthetic traditions—or simply do not know haiku in English. Haiku is a poetry of simplicity and suggestion new to Western literature. It has been called "the wordless poem,"[6] and is often so bare as to seem meaningless to the uninitiated. Yet its few words have such an ontological immediacy that the sensitive reader can almost reach out and touch the things they describe. However commonplace the image, it is *now* in one of those timeless moments when it flashes forth an unspoken message of the oneness of existence. It does so in the silence that surrounds the words. Blyth has called haiku "an open door which looks shut," because it takes an intuitive awareness to see that moment of perception which lies just over the threshold. The reader must be an equal partner in the creative process—the slightest shift of focus or mood can close the door again. Aware readers are increasing, however, and the "visibility" of haiku in English will depend on their perception.

Haiku in English is still in the process of finding its "way." Beyond a general agreement that haiku should be short, concise, and immediate (or brief, simple, and direct, etc.), individual poets may often diverge widely in their conceptions of what a haiku is and how one is created. One of the most fundamental questions raised about haiku has been: is it basically a religious or an esthetic experience?

[6] By Alan Watts. Eric Amann wrote an exceptionally fine book on haiku using this phrase for the title. It appeared as a special issue of *Haiku* in 1969.

A number of those who favor the religious, or as some prefer to say, spiritual, side of this question relate haiku to the philosophy of Zen. J. W. Hackett and Eric Amann have been spokesmen for this view, which follows the "teachings" of R. H. Blyth. Citing Bashō—"Haiku is simply what is happening in this place, at this moment"— Hackett emphasizes haiku as a "way" of life, rather than as literature. In his book, *The Way of Haiku* (1969),[7] the poet states:

> I have written in the conviction that the best haiku are created from direct and immediate experience with nature, and that this intuitive experience can be expressed in any language. In essence I regard haiku as fundamentally existential and experiential, rather than literary. There are, of course, important structural and artistic considerations involved in the expression of the haiku experience . . .

In *Haiku in English* (1965), Henderson contrasts Hackett's approach ("what may loosely be called the Bashō school") with that of Nicholas Virgilio and others who stress imaginative creation—that is, the artistic role of the poet as a maker of imagined scenes as well as experienced ones, exemplified in Japanese haiku by Buson. Some poets who lean toward this view may believe their work is ultimately based on actual experience too, in the sense that even their imagined scenes are put together from things they have known. And since it is possible for *readers* to experience a "haiku moment" through words,

[7] One of the very few haiku poets with a book readily obtainable at bookstores, Hackett alone has had a large body of work available for several years. A number of the poets in this anthology have, however, been published by small presses (see Appendix B: Biographies).

even though they may never have encountered it in reality, there are poets who claim they can *discover* such moments in words during the creative process.

There is also the question of "natural speech" (artless) as opposed to language which uses poetic techniques. An argument against a too "literary" approach is R. H. Blyth's admonition that a bejewelled finger distracts from what it is pointing at. But it is well to keep in mind that a deformed finger can be distracting too, and may even point the wrong way.

The distinction between haiku and senryu, which are structurally similar, has also been a subject of controversy. Haiku is said to relate human nature to nature in general, while senryu is concerned primarily with human nature and is often humorous; but it is hard to draw the line.[8]

There are other differences among the haiku poets: there are the 5-7-5ers who believe haiku should be written in three lines of 5-7-5 syllables; then there are those who think the norm for English should be less than seventeen syllables to more closely approximate the actual length of seventeen Japanese *jion* (symbol-sounds),[9] which are generally shorter than English syllables. Still others, like Michael McClintock, are for a "liberated haiku"—rejecting syllable-counting completely. There is the problem of subjectivity in haiku: is it allowable at all, and if so to what degree? And, on the other hand, is complete objectivity really possible?—and so on.

These "disputes" among the poets don't prevent them from appreciating each other's work, and are actually a way of answering Henderson's call to "work out our

---

[8] I have not tried to separate the senryu from the haiku in this book, though I'm sure there are a few that would be considered senryu even by their authors.

[9] See Appendix A for definitions suggested by the Haiku Society for "haiku" and related terms.

own standards." "Haiku" may be on its way to becoming a much broader term than it has been in the past. This may or may not be a good thing; but while some are working to broaden the concept, there are others who are moving toward a simpler, purer, deeper kind of haiku—and even a few who are finding ways to create poems which do both at once. Japanese haiku has survived countless controversies in its centuries-old history and haiku in English will too. As Henderson says, what haiku in English will become "will depend primarily on the poets who write them."[10]

A great diversity lies in the pages ahead. But though these poets are all moving along individual paths, they are all following the haiku "way." The variety of their voices should delight us as much as the oneness they reveal enlightens us. For the joy of life is to be able to see it anew each moment. These haiku moments await only your contribution of awareness.

Here you'll find the strange landscapes of Nicholas Virgilio, which, while remaining part of the real world, take us on a surrealistic trip to the source of the life force in a lily or to the mystery of death in the headlights of a funeral procession; or the simple wonders of J. W. Hackett, where a caterpillar or a small cloud of gnats can take us to the core of existence simply by being what they are *now;* the daring experimentation of William J. Higginson or Anita Virgil, who both find new visceral possibilities in words; the muse-guided nature sensitivity of Mabelsson Norway, whose word-spells can call trees and rocks out of a timeless mist; the pure simplicity of Robert Spiess, the subtle clarity of whose images resonates again and again through the natural juxtaposition of the barest aspects of nature; the rich, fertile earth and living waters of John Wills; the haunting silences of

[10] *Haiku in English.*

Foster Jewell; the fresh virtuosity, sensual vigor, and delicacy of perception of Michael McClintock; and many more, all with their own individual voices, their own way of looking at the world through haiku.

There are undoubtedly poets and haiku missing from the following pages that belong here, but here at least is a representative selection—here is haiku in English becoming visible.

New York City
June 1973

BOOKS MENTIONED

Amann, Eric W. *The Wordless Poem.* Haiku Magazine, Toronto, 1969.

Blyth, R. H. *Haiku.* Hokuseido, Tokyo, 1949–52. 4 volumes.

Brower, Gary. *Haiku in Western Languages.* Scarecrow Press, Inc., Metuchen, N.J., 1972.

Hackett, J. W. *The Way of Haiku.* Japan Publications, Inc., Tokyo, 1969.

Henderson, Harold G. *The Bamboo Broom.* Houghton Mifflin Company, Boston, 1934.

———. *Haiku in English.* Japan Society, New York, 1965. (Republished by Charles E. Tuttle Co., Inc., Rutland, Vt., and Tokyo, 1967.)

———. *An Introduction to Haiku.* Doubleday & Company, Inc., Garden City, N.Y., 1958.

Yasuda, Kenneth. *The Japanese Haiku.* Charles E. Tuttle Co., Inc., Rutland, Vt., and Tokyo, 1957.

———. *A Pepper Pod.* Alfred A. Knopf, Inc., New York, 1947.

ALSO RECOMMENDED

Blyth, R. H. *A History of Haiku*. Hokuseido, Tokyo, 1963–64. 2 volumes.

Ichikawa, Sanki (ed.). *Haikai and Haiku*. Nippon Gakujutsu Shinkokai, Tokyo, 1958.

Ueda, Makoto. *Literary and Art Theories in Japan*. The Press of Case Western Reserve University, Cleveland, 1967.

———. *Matsuo Basho*. Twayne Publishers, Inc., New York, 1970.

MAGAZINES

Haiku, Eric Amann, editor 1967–71, will become editor again in 1974, 61 Macdonell Avenue, Toronto, Ontario, Canada M6R 2A3.

Haiku West, Leroy Kanterman, editor, c/o Japan Society, 333 East 47 Street, New York, N.Y. 10017.

Modern Haiku, Kay Titus Mormino, editor, 414 N. Orange Drive, Los Angeles, Calif. 90036.

Dragonfly: A Quarterly of Haiku Highlights, Lorraine Ellis Harr, editor, 4102 N.E. 130th Place, Portland, Ore. 97230.

HAIKU SOCIETY OF AMERICA, c/o Japan Society, 333 East 47 Street, New York, N.Y. 10017.

THE
HAIKU
ANTHOLOGY

Mary Acosta

dark summer lake
with but one rower
unlit cabins

Eric Amann

Snow falling
on the empty parking-lot:
Christmas Eve . . .

Billboards . . .
    wet
        in spring
            rain . . .

The circus tent
all folded up:
October mist . . .

Jack Cain

an empty elevator
opens
closes

waiting:
dry snowflakes fall
against the headlights

someone's newspaper
drifts with the snow
at 4 a.m.

empty room:
one swinging coat hanger
measures the silence

l.a. davidson

beyond
stars beyond
star

Frances Drivas

morning
in green shade only the green
statue staring
out to sea

Bernard Lionel Einbond

The white of her neck
   as she lifts her hair for me
   to undo her dress.

Larry Gates

The killdeer
    unmoved
        as the surf passes his feet.

Misty rain falling
   on Lookout Mountain . . .
      the silent cannons.

On the jewelweed
sparkling raindrops are falling
from blossom to blossom.

At the river-bend
   wriggling towards the setting sun
   a lone watersnake.

As   a   flashes
the   little   white
falls   water-thrush
darken

J. W. Hackett

Searching on the wind,
the hawk's cry . . .
is the shape of its beak.

A bitter morning:
   sparrows sitting together
   without any necks.

The fleeing sandpipers
turn about suddenly
and chase back the sea!

Time after time
    caterpillar climbs this broken stem,
        then probes beyond.

Wind sounds through the trees . . .
while here, gnats play in the calm
of wooded sunlight.

Moon fades into dawn . . .
an ivory moth settles
within the lily.

Deep within the stream
    the huge fish lie motionless,
    facing the current.

An old spider web
    low above the forest floor,
        sagging full of seeds.

The stillness of dawn:
  crashing between the branches,
    a solitary leaf.

William J. Higginson

a robin listens
then flies off
snow eddies

Holding the water,
    held by it—
        the dark mud.

More intricate
   than all winter's designs,
      this spring flake.

Interstices

sky-black gull
                        skims
    the wave inland
against the cliff
                        whitens

                                high tide—
                                every now and then
                                driftwood
                                rocks

                        the ducks land
                        and turn on the swells
                        to face the wind

evening star
almost within
the moon's half-curve

caterpillar
atop the rock
the rising tide

A sudden flash;
    the road ahead is empty.
    Summer thunder.

from ETUDES FOR EASTRE, 1972

hard fall

slowly
checking
the un-
sheathed
          axe

before the descent
musing then seeing
the sudden bluebird

Gary Hotham

Deserted tennis court.
wind through the net.

Pheasant
at the town dump
this winter day . . .

Sunset dying
on the end of a rusty
beer can . . .

Stalled car.
    foot tracks being filled
        with snow.

Crows gather
on a distant grove
of bare cherry trees . . .

Clement Hoyt

Hair, in my comb's teeth
the color of autumn wind—
this whole day is gray.

In that empty house,
  with broken windows rattling,
    a door slams and slams.

Leaves moil in the yard,
    reveal an eyeless doll's head . . .
        slowly conceal it.

A Hallowe'en mask,
   floating face up in the ditch,
   slowly shakes its head.

In that lightning flash—
through the night rain—I saw
. . . whatever it was.

Foster Jewell

Cliff dweller ruins,
and the silence of swallows
encircling silence.

On snowshoes today—
walking over fences
and a world not there.

As dead limbs fall,
just these shadows left in snow,
showing the places.

Left on mountain wall—
down over the balsams—
the snowfall—the falls.

Cows paw at the snow—
turn—and seeing what I am,
go on foraging.

Somewhere behind me,
seeming in dark-silence
to feel a slow coiling.

Under ledges
and looking for the coolness
that keeps touching my face.

Where the coyote called,
rising in full cry, the moon . . .
the sound of silence.

Nearing the mountain
yesterday, and still today . . .
tomorrow.

Some unknown sound . . .
the looking behind me—
the looking all around.

Disturbing some brush
and after miles and miles . . .
still the rattling sound.

From this waterfall
another river rises,
weaving off in mist.

That breeze brought it—
a moment of moonlight
to the hidden fern.

Fall wind in pinyons . . .
Faster and louder patters
yesterday's shower.

Finding this cavern—
following the lantern light . . .
followed by silence.

Leroy Kanterman

Moored to its pilings,
the rusting ferryboat
rides the morning tide . . .

Julia Rankin King

From the mountain, thunder . . .
a small wind lifts the branches
lets them fall again

Elizabeth Searle Lamb

Broken kite, sprawled
    on a sand dune, its line caught
  in the beach plum . . .

Geraldine Clinton Little

Fallen horse—
flies hovering
in the vulture's shadow

David Lloyd

Moonlit sleet
In the holes of my
Harmonica

At the bottom
Of the rocky mountain slope,
A pile of pebbles

Duck feathers
On the lake's shore—
Silent skies

Wild rose bending—
And bending even more
With the bee's weight

The mosquito
Filling up with blood—
And a full moon!

Michael McClintock

dead cat . . .
open-mouthed
to the pouring rain

from TEHACHAPI DESERT

glimmering morning
silence unfolds all
the yucca

across the sands
the rippling quiet
cloud shadow

in the night
the wind
shifting rocks . . .

from DEATH VALLEY

a side-canyon:
pausing a moment, listening
into its reach . . .

letting my tongue
  deeper into the cool
    ripe tomato

summer afternoon:
watching the sun move
in a water-drop

a broken window
reflects half the moon,
half of me

a grasshopper
jumped into it:
summer dusk

hearing
   cockroach feet;
      the midnight snowfall

overtaken
by a single cloud,
and letting it pass . . .

rowing downstream
red leaves   swirling
behind me

the leaf
falls . . .
fluttering sunlight

pushing
    inside . . . until
        her teeth shine

                    the first melt . . .
                        her eyes gone
                            under their lids

while we wait
to do it again,
the rains of spring

she leaves—
　　warm pillow scent
　　remaining

peering out
the scarecrow's ear—
two glittering eyes

twisting inland,
the sea fog takes awhile
in the apple trees

long summer day . . .
my neighbor's bull,
at it again

a single tulip!
hopelessly,
i passed on

from VIETNAM

Hamburger Hill . . .
the full moon
in our eyes

a drizzling rain . . .
washing their blood
into their blood

tonight . . . wishing
the lightning were lightning,
the thunder, thunder

pond lilies . . .
    moving with the ripples
    that never reach them

a poppy . . .
a field of poppies!
the hills blowing with poppies!

Mabelsson Norway

The old rooster crows...
Out of the mist come the rocks
and the twisted pine

One breaker crashes...
  As the next draws up, a lull—
    and sandpiper-cries

The waves now fall short
of the stranded jellyfish...
In it shines the sky

Down to dark leaf-mold
the falling dogwood-petal
carries its moonlight

Still sunlit, one tree...
Into the mountain-shadow
it lets fall a leaf

On the top fence-rail
she lights, knocking off some snow—
a common sparrow

With blue-shadowed snow
deep in the log-hut's windows—
the setting sun's glow

At the window, sleet...
Here in the darkening hut—
sudden squeaks of mice

SEQUENCE XV

Overwhelmed by mist
  the rocky peak struggles out—
    and sinks back under

My snow down her neck
  my sister laughs, and shudders,
    and kisses my mouth

Staining the cliff dark
  with afternoon meltwater—
    a cornice of snow

SEQUENCE XV: concluded

Lodged in the plunge-pool
the trunk of a broken tree
parts the waterfall

Under the cool pines
the path dips round a boulder
and climbs to a ledge

By her childhood name
I call and call my sister—
and so do the cliffs

Across the still lake
 through upcurls of morning mist—
  the cry of a loon!

A patter of rain...
The lily-pad undulates
on widening rings

On a leaf, a leaf
    casts a swaying green shadow—
    and the tree-frog sings!

Now the leaves are still—
and only the mockingbird
lets the moonlight through!

Gleaming—sunken stones...
With her shadow, the catfish
turns them off and on

Now the leaves are still—
　　and only the mockingbird
　　　　lets the moonlight through!

Gleaming—sunken stones...
With her shadow, the catfish
turns them off and on

Down the coral slope
   disappearing in the gloom—
   a pale yellow fish

In the sea, sunset...
   On the dark dune, a bright fringe
   of waving grasses

In the garden pool,
    dark and still, a stepping-stone
  releases the moon

Steadily it snows...
   Under the shadowy pines—
   where are the shadows?

Snow-laden bushes—
  one bent to the ground, and one
swaying in the wind

Alan Pizzarelli

the fat lady
bends over the tomatoes
a full moon

tonite
nothing to write

but this

a spark
falls to the ground
             darkens

thats it

Marjory Bates Pratt

Not a breath of air—
only a water bug mars
the pine's reflection.

Sydell Rosenberg

In the laundermat
    she peers into the machine
    as the sun goes down.

Michael Segers

in the eggshell after the chick has hatched

Ron Seitz

so high in the sky

                              just

    a black speck

                    fluttering

the   lone   autumn   bird

Robert Spiess

Winter moon;
a beaver lodge in the marsh,
mounded with snow

Blue jays in the pines;
  the northern river's ledges
  cased with melting ice

Misting rain;
in a redbud on the bank
a yellow warbler

Dry, summer day;
   chalk-white plover mute
      on a mid-stream rock

Tar paper cabin
    behind the river's white birch
      —a muskellunge leaps

A light river wind;
on the crannied cliff
hang harebell and fern

Muttering thunder . . .
the bottom of the river
scattered with clams

Marsh marigold
  on a low island of grass;
    the warmth of the sun

Shooting the rapids!
—a glimpse of a meadow
gold with buttercups

Lean-to of tin;
   a pintail on the river
     in the pelting rain

Wispy autumn clouds;
in the river shallows
the droppings of a deer

An autumn morning;
a deer in the shrouding mist
fords the shallow stream

Dawn over the stream;
a milkweed seed drifting through
a pillar of gnats

Ostrich fern on shore;
  a short-eared owl in an oak
    watching the canoe

A long wedge of geese;
  straw-gold needles of the larch
    on the flowing stream

Bonnie Squires

dead cat
  frozen to winter ground
   prying her off

Jan S. Streif

Lonely night:—
  the elephant
    tugs at his chain.

Tom Tico

A wisp of spring cloud
  drifting apart from the rest . . .
  slowly evaporates.

A wandering path . . .
only my grinding footsteps
and the birds' silence.

After gazing at stars . . .
    now, I adjust to the rocks
    under my sleeping bag.

James Tipton

the old barber
sweeping hair
into the giant bag

Cor van den Heuvel

high above the city
dawn flares
from a window-washer's pail

above the clear water
still in shadow
the sunlight just touches

a floating sponge

on the car bumper
a long landscape
unwinds

in the hotel lobby
the bare bulb of a floor lamp
shines down on its distant base

tundra

an empty wheelchair
rolls
in from the waves

in front of the newsstand
a spring wind
ripples the Sunday funnies

behind the station
the setting sun shines
under the wheels of a boxcar

a gun belt
with empty holster
hangs on the back of the chair

in the water-tank dark
behind the toilet
a slime coated copper ball   floats

an empty passenger train
stands on a siding
frost on all its windows

through the small holes
in the mailbox
sunlight on a blue stamp

the windshield-wipers
vanish over the horizon
Geronimo leaps to his horse

Anita Virgil

The black spaces:
as much star
as star!

Awakening . . .
the cold fresh scent:
new snow.

walking the snow-crust
      not sinking
          sinking

Emerging hot and rosy
from their skins—
beets!

not seeing
the room is white
until that red apple

grass path lasts
the bird's
foot
long as

in the damp spring evening
blackbirds
changing trees

a phoebe's cry . . .
the blue shadows
on the dinner plates

the dark
throbbing
with spring
peepers

morning bath
clouds & birds float between
still wet limbs

Quiet afternoon:
water shadows
on the pine bark.

a white bird
running on the shade
of the zebra's legs

the swan's head
turns away from sunset
to his dark side

the last blackbird creaks
over
into night

trickling
over the dam—
summer's end

Nicholas Virgilio

Lily:
    out of the water . . .
      out of itself.

Heat before the storm:
a fly disturbs the quiet
of the empty store.

Lone red-winged blackbird
riding a reed in high tide—
billowing clouds.

Now the swing is still:
  a suspended tire
    centers the autumn moon.

Deep in rank grass,
  through a bullet-riddled helmet:
  an unknown flower.

*—In Memory of Corporal
Lawrence J. Virgilio, USMC*

Into the blinding sun . . .
the funeral procession's
glaring headlights.

Autumn twilight:
the wreath on the door
lifts in the wind.

The empty highway:
a tiger swallowtail
follows the divider.

The town clock's face
   adds another shade of yellow
      to the afterglow.

A distant balloon
   drifting over the county fair,
      eclipses the moon.

The cathedral bell
  is shaking a few snowflakes
  from the morning air.

The first snowfall
   is coating a small stack
      of rusty cannon balls.

The sack of kittens
sinking in the icy creek,
increases the cold.

Shaking the muskrat—
    snow falls from the trapper's hair—
    and from a reed.

A crow in the snowy pine . . .
   inching up a branch,
      letting the evening sun through.

Gerald Robert Vizenor

Mounds of foam
Beneath the waterfall
Floating silently.

Fireflies blinking
One alights then disappears
In the dewy grass.

Upon the pine cones
First flakes of delicate snow
Becoming drops of dew.

Larry Wiggin

crickets . . .
then
thunder

wind:
the long hairs
on my neck

dreaming . . .
dust
on the window

Rod Willmot

Listening . . .
After a while,
I take up my axe again

If I go alone,
I'll lie in the wildflowers
    and dream of you

A page of Shelley
brightens and dims
             with passing clouds

Breathing . . .
the teacup
filled with shadow

May rain . . .
On the sill, a feather
        shifts in the draught

A quiet rustle
    through the leaves . . .
stirring together in our sleep

A small noise . . .
papers uncrumpling.
stillness again

John Wills

the moon at dawn
        lily pads blow white
in a sudden breeze

within the spring
   a dappled crawfish backs
      among the cresses

a mayfly
        struggles down the stream
                one wing flapping dry

the glitter
of the gravel bed
this morning

clouds
slide down the river
under swallows

a bluegill rises
to the match   wavers
and falls away

where the waters
come together tumble
        under the logs

the river pools
among the rocks, then pools
and pools again

another river
        somewhere down
        inside me

below the falls
a leaping trout   scatters
the morning mist

river
just at twilight moving off
in rain

another bend
then at last   the moon
and all the stars

The forest
stands so straight and tall
at noon!

all at once
a dragonfly   hanging
above the horsetails

The hills
　release the summer clouds
　　one . . . by one . . . by one . . .

boulders
just beneath the boat . . .
it's dawn

beyond the porch
the summer night . . . leaning out
a moment

Beyond the pumpkins,
  matching fold for fold . . .
    the orange moon.

November evening—
  the faintest tick of snow
  upon the cornstalks.

Late winter dawn . . .
  Between the snow and snow . . .
    the pencilled woods.

In an upstairs room
    of the abandoned farmhouse
    a doll moon-gazing.

Kenneth Yasuda

The shadow of the trees
Almost reaches to my desk
With the summer breeze.

A crimson dragonfly,
As it lights, sways together
With a leaf of rye.

A crimson dragonfly,
Glancing the water, casts rings
As it passes by.

Virginia Brady Young

During a downpour,
the frog's eyes
—open

Ridges of snow
   holding
      rain

On the first day of spring
snow falling
from one bough to another

In a circle of thaw
the cat walks
round and round

fallen birch leaf
vein-side
to the sky

The silence
in moonlight
of stones

APPENDIXES A & B

Appendix A: Definitions

The following letter and proposed definitions were prepared for submission to publishers of English dictionaries by the Haiku Society of America and are used with their permission.

Haiku Society of America

In those unabridged English dictionaries where the words haiku, haikai, and hokku have been listed, not one of the definitions given has been wholly accurate or even passably satisfactory.

This is not surprising inasmuch as there is no such thing as an unabridged Japanese dictionary from which the definitions could have been taken. Nevertheless, the vast increase of interest in haiku which has occurred in the last decade suggests that the English language dictionaries should give authoritative definitions for these words.

Such definitions are not easy and require study. In the first place, a distinction should be made between haiku and hokku. *Hokku* is an old Japanese word applicable to more than one kind of verse, including what is now called haiku. Circa 1890 the Japanese poet Masaoka Shiki proposed that the term *haiku* be used to designate that particular kind of Japanese poetry that has aroused such interest in America, England, and elsewhere. His proposal met with success, and in Japan the word *hokku* is obsolete as applied to this kind of poetry.

The definition of haiku has been made more difficult by the fact that many uninformed persons have considered it to be a "form" like a sonnet or a triolet (17 syllables, divided 5, 7, and 5). That it is not simply a "form" is amply demonstrated by the fact that the Japanese differentiate *haiku* from *senryu*—a type of verse (or poem) that has exactly the same "form" as *haiku* but differs in content from it. Actually, there is no rigid "form" for Japanese *haiku*. Seventeen Japanese *jion* (symbol-sounds)* is the norm, but some 5% of "classical" *haiku* depart from it, and so do a still greater percentage of "modern" Japanese *haiku*. To the Japanese and to American haiku poets, it is the content and not the form alone that makes a haiku.

Hence, we present for your consideration the following proposed definitions for haiku and related words: haikai, hokku, and senryu. (The latter, though its use is as yet less widespread than that of haiku, is rapidly coming into the English language.)

Respectfully,

Harold G. Henderson
HONORARY PRESIDENT

William J. Higginson
Anita Virgil
COMMITTEE ON DEFINITIONS

PRELIMINARY NOTE

1. Though it was our original intention to confine ourselves to the discussion of haiku, we found it impossible to do this adequately without also covering the

* See PRELIMINARY NOTE #2.

terms haikai, hokku, and senryu. By use of cross-referencing, we hope that we have been able to present a clear picture of the meaning of haiku in the briefest manner possible.

2. The Japanese words *jion* (symbol-sound) and *onji* (sound-symbol) have been mistranslated into English as "syllable" for many years. However, in most Japanese poetry the *jion* or *onji* does not correspond to the Western notion of syllable. For example, while each of the entry words is reckoned as two syllables in English, "hokku" and "haiku" are each counted as three *jion*, while "haikai" and "senryu" each have four *jion*. On the other hand, where each Japanese *jion* is equal and brief as "do, re, mi, etc.," English single syllables can vary greatly in time duration. (For a further discussion of the Japanese sound system see Roy Andrew Miller, *The Japanese Language*.)

3. Each of the four entry words is its own plural.

HAIKU

(1) An unrhymed Japanese poem recording the essence of a moment keenly perceived, in which Nature is linked to human nature. It usually consists of seventeen† *jion* (Japanese symbol-sounds).

(2) A foreign adaptation of (1). It is usually written in three lines of five, seven, and five syllables. (See also HAIKAI, HOKKU.)

NOTE to (2):

That part of the definition which begins "It is usually written" places a heavy weight on the word "usually."

† Divided into three parts of 5-7-5. (Editor's Note)

We depend on that word to provide latitude for variations in syllable count and in number of lines or other external aspects of "form" *providing* they meet the primary stringent requirements expressed in the first part of the definition. Though 17 syllables is still the norm in English language haiku, it is more and more common for a haiku to consist of *fewer* syllables. Rarely is a haiku longer than 17 syllables.

While all Japanese classical *haiku*, as well as most modern ones, contain a *kigo* (season-word: a word or phrase indicating one of the four seasons of their year), extreme variations of climate in the U.S.A. make it impossible to put a recognizable "season-word" into every American haiku. Therefore, American adaptations are not so concerned with season words as are most Japanese *haiku*.

HOKKU

(1) The first stanza of a Japanese linked-verse poem (see HAIKAI).
(2) (Obsolete) A haiku.

NOTE to (2):

Hokku was used as a synonym for haiku by the Imagist poets, but is obsolete in modern American usage. It is definitely obsolete today in Japan.

SENRYU

(1) A Japanese poem structurally similar to the Japanese *haiku* (which see), but primarily concerned with human nature. It is usually humorous or satiric.
(2) A foreign adaptation of (1).
(3) Loosely, a poem similar to haiku which does not meet the criteria for haiku.

(1) A type of Japanese linked-verse poem, popular from the fifteenth through the nineteenth centuries. Such a poem normally consists of thirty-six, fifty, or one hundred stanzas, alternating seventeen and fourteen‡ *jion* (Japanese symbol-sounds). Usually a small group of poets took turns composing the poem's stanzas, whose content and grammar were governed by fairly complex rules.

NOTES:

In Japanese, the word *haikai* is commonly used as an abbreviation for the phrase *haikai no renga,* usually translated as "comic linked-verse." Under the influence of Bashō (1644–1694) the tone of *haikai no renga* became more serious, but the name was retained.

The word *haikai* is also used in Japanese as a general term for all haiku-related literature (haiku, *haikai no renga,* the diaries of haiku poets, etc.).

In Spanish and French the word *haikai* is often used to refer to either the Japanese *haiku* or Western adaptations of the Japanese *haiku.* However, in modern Japanese usage, reference to a single *haikai* is to a *haikai no renga.*

‡ Divided 5-7-5 and 7-7. (Editor's Note)

Appendix B: Biographies

The following "biographies" are for the most part auto-biographical sketches written for this book at the editor's request.

Mary Acosta

"Born Mary Jane Milunec on November 28, 1922, in Maspeth, Long Island, New York. Attended Cooper Union Day Art School. B.S. in Art Education, New York University, 1959. Artist: one-man show at Beaux Arts Gallery, Pinellas Park, Florida, 1971. Prizes in poetry (4th of July Festival of Florida State Poetry, 1971) and ceramics (1st Gallery Art Exhibition—Miami Art Center, 1972).

"I've always had a keen interest in oriental art, especially screen paintings, and in Zen philosophy—which I believe is at the heart of haiku—but I learned of haiku itself mainly through the haiku magazines."

Eric Amann

"Born January 16, 1938, Munich. First interest in haiku started over ten years ago through reading the six volumes of R. H. Blyth. Started experimenting with English language haiku ca. 1965, issued the first Canadian haiku magazine in spring of 1967, called *Haiku*, now in its seventh year, making it the longest surviving quarterly dedicated to haiku in the Western hemisphere. Published *The Wordless Poem: A Study of Zen in Haiku* in 1969. Will be publishing a collection of my haiku in 1974."

Jack Cain

"Born December 16, 1940, near Toronto, Canada. Raised in the country and attended a one-room public school. Began writing haiku near Ungava Bay in the Arctic in the summer of 1962. Have written little since beginning a journey to the East in 1970."

l.a. davidson

"Poetry has been a continuing part of my life since youth on a ranch in Montana, where I was born long enough ago to have acquired a husband and two daughters (now married), for whom I have been a homemaker in various places, most recently in Greenwich Village.

"From 1966, when a friend encouraged me to become involved with it, a substantial part of my free time has been spent studying, reading, writing, revising, and thinking haiku. That special evocative and elusive quality that is haiku pipes me to pursue."

Frances Drivas

"Born 1917 on the Lower East Side in Manhattan and attended schools in New York City. Now reside in Brooklyn. First came across haiku at an early age in a poetry handbook. Became interested in the Japanese and their culture through contact with them in business and art, but it was not until the formation of the Haiku Society of America that haiku became a subject of serious study."

Bernard Lionel Einbond

"Born May 19, 1937, in New York City and educated at Columbia (A.B. '58), I was just old enough to be among the last of those generations of Columbia student poets to receive the encouragement of the late Professor Mark Van Doren. My poetry (haiku and non-haiku) has been appearing in magazines since 1960 and is included in the books *Live Poetry* (Holt, Rinehart & Winston, 1971) and *Invention* (Winthrop, 1973).

"Like many others, I first became familiar with haiku through Harold G. Henderson's *An Introduction to Haiku,* although I suppose I had always known Ezra Pound's "In a Station of the Metro." I prefer to think of haiku as a verse form, and most of my own haiku are of seventeen syllables, broken into three lines of five, seven, and five."

Larry Gates

"I was born in Chicago on June 12, 1942. My first introduction to haiku came in a creative writing class at Eastern Illinois University in 1962. Since then I have been a fairly regular contributor to English-language haiku periodicals. Though much of my haiku is rather traditional in both form and content, I have experimented with concrete haiku and writing haiku with the aid of a computer. Currently (1973) I am working as an assistant professor of psychology at the University of Southern Mississippi. My purpose in writing haiku is not so much to express my own poetic feelings as it is to evoke poetic feelings in others."

255

James William Hackett

Born August 6, 1929, in Seattle, Washington.

"I discovered haiku through the writings of R. H. Blyth and Alan Watts in 1954, but it wasn't until after a near fatal accident in the late 1950s that I began to live and write it. For I was reborn from this experience, with my outlook and values profoundly changed. The culture and learning which I had valued faded into insignificance, while living Now—aware of this present of life and the glory of greater nature—became all-important to me. Haiku alone, of all the arts, could best express my new-found love of life: its emphasis upon moment and selfless devotion to suchness (nature just as it is) was precisely what I had come to feel so deeply. Haiku became not just a form of literature or a literary pursuit, but a Way of living awareness, an art of Zen. Although I was trained in Western philosophy, the philosophical values of Taoism and Zen have always been the basis and reason for my poetry, and thus I regard the quality of *muga* (non-ego) as inseparable from, and indispensable to, living the way of haiku.

"R. H. Blyth had the most influence upon my writing and its development: his encouragement and his spiritual emphasis were invaluable. And my many years of correspondence with Harold Henderson proved most stimulating. Despite (and because of) these influences I remain a fiercely independent spirit. In recent years I have been writing longer forms of nature poetry similar to those of the Chinese.

"My poems have appeared in several haiku magazines, in R. H. Blyth's *A History of Haiku*, Vol. II, in Harold G. Henderson's *Haiku in English*, and more recently in textbooks and anthologies in the United States, Canada, and England. They have been heard on American radio and the BBC. My books of poetry include *The Way of Haiku*, *Bug Haiku*, and *Haiku Poetry*, Vols. 1–4. All are published by Japan Publications, Inc., Tokyo/San Francisco."

William J. Higginson

"Born in New York City, December 1938, raised in the Bronx and Bergenfield, New Jersey. After high school, MIT for two years, then joined the Air Force. While in AF went to Yale's Institute of Far Eastern Languages; honors in Japanese, 1960. Introduced there to Bashō's poem *furuike ya / kawazu tobikomu / mizu no oto*. Appreciation and attempts to translate it led to serious study of the Japanese haiku while serving in Japan, 1961–63. More study after returning to U.S. and civilian life resulted in *Twenty-Five Pieces of Now: Classical Japanese Haiku with English Translations* (New Haven, Conn., 1968) under the pseudonym Hian. In 1967 discovered the little magazines devoted to haiku in English; a number of essays, reviews, translations, and original haiku were accepted beginning 1968, particularly in Eric W. Amann's *Haiku Magazine*, Toronto. In October 1968, joined with Harold G. Henderson, Leroy Kanterman, and others to form the Haiku Society of America. A series of articles in *Haiku Highlights*, edited by Jean Calkins, resulted in her publishing my *Itadakimasu: Essays on Haiku and Senryu in English* (Kanona, N.Y.: J & C Transcripts, 1971). At Eric Amann's invitation, took over editing *Haiku Magazine* 1971–73, continuing his policy of encouraging experimentation, and opening the magazine to more general poetry. Under the aegis of the magazine, a bibliography of haiku materials in English, *Haiku Checklist*, will be out early 1974. *thistle brilliant morning*, translations of haiku by the modern Japanese poets Shiki, Hekigodō, Santōka, and Hōsai, was published as a special issue of *Byways*, fall 1973, edited by Gerry Loose in Arkesden, England. Non-haiku poems and translations have appeared in a few other magazines, notably *Madrona*. Other current work includes getting From Here Press off the ground and translating Lao Tzu's *Tao Teh Ching* from the Chinese. Presently living in Paterson, New Jersey.

"In addition to those mentioned above, influences have been Ezra Pound, William Carlos Williams, Cid Corman's translations, Bernhard Karlgren and the laconism of classical

Chinese (which I hope to re-create in my translations, as it has not yet been done), Denise Levertov, Federico García Lorca, Makoto Ueda and the Japanese *renga*, J. S. Bach and Béla Bartók."

Gary Hotham

"I was born on 28 July 1950 in Presque Isle, Maine, and have lived on a potato farm in the general vicinity for the greater part of my life. I received a B.A. in History from the University of Maine in 1972. I also attended Westminster Theological Seminary (Philadelphia) for a summer session and fall semester. Am presently (1973) a research analyst for the USAF.

"I became interested in haiku six or seven years ago. I find it a powerful form of poetry to read and try to write, and am grateful to the Japanese for creating it."

Clement Hoyt

(Clement Hoyt died in 1970. The following biographical sketch is by his wife, Violet Hoyt:)

"Clement Hoyt was born May 14, 1906, in Houston, Texas. He attended Proso School, Houston; Kempner Military Academy; Hill School, Pottstown, Pennsylvania; and the University of Alabama.

"His interest in haiku began in 1936 when he became a pupil of Nyogen Senzaki, a Japanese poet, calligrapher, lecturer, author, and Zen master. Clement, who had written all forms of poetry since his teens, was fascinated with haiku and wrote many of them as exercises in his Zen studies. He edited and published *American Haiku* for one year, 1964 (Volume II, Nos. 1 and 2).

"For eight and a half years before 1959, when he sold out and retired, he published and edited four weekly newspapers of his own. Prior to that he had his own advertising agency for several years. Before that he was a typical footloose journalist—edited two trade journals, worked on several dailies, and free-lanced for magazines."

Foster Jewell

Born July 21, 1893, in Grand Rapids, Michigan.

"My actual haiku experience began with writing a few pieces in the 5/7/5 pattern for the first issue of our poetry publication (SCTH) in March of 1964. At that time I was interested in 'Zen,' and reading D. T. Suzuki.

"However, from 1956 to 1958 I was living in a remote section of the Arkansas Ozarks, tramping the woods in search of black walnut suitable for sculpture—a helpful exercise, also, in awareness of the processes and manifestations taking place in field and forest, and from which came my first book of verses, *Strato Lanes in Star Grass*, Sangre de Cristo Press, 1959.

"I began to submit haiku to *American Haiku* in 1965, and won eight of the monthly awards. In '69 through '72 Sangre de Cristo Press (now at 1325 Cabrillo Avenue, #12, Venice, California 90291) published my four books of haiku: *Sand Waves, Beachcomber, Haiku Sketches*, and *Mirage*. I have contributed to Eric Amann's *Haiku*, to *Modern Haiku, Haiku West*, and *Haiku Highlights* (now *Dragonfly*)."

Leroy Kanterman

Born: October 2, 1923, in New York City.

"An interest in Zen in the late fifties led to haiku in 1959. *Haiku West* was conceived in 1966, publication starting in June 1967. With Mr. Henderson, without whose help the idea would have remained just that, started the Haiku Society of America in the summer of 1968.

"In late 1967, I published a small collection of haiku & senryu of mine under the title *The Ram's Horn*."

Julia Rankin King

"I was born in Los Angeles in 1939. Have just finished a Bachelor's in Art History at St. Louis University, and am beginning Doctoral work at the same school in Historical Theology. I began to experiment with haiku while studying Taoism and Japanese Buddhism. In a number of my haiku I have worked with impressions drawn from a childhood spent in California's Sierra Nevada."

Elizabeth Searle Lamb

"Born January 22, 1917, in Topeka, Kansas; Bachelor of Arts and Bachelor of Music degrees, University of Kansas; married in 1941 to F. Bruce Lamb, forester and writer; a daughter, Carolyn. Traveled through much of Central and South America, living in Trinidad, B.W.I., Honduras, Brazil, Panama, Colombia, and Puerto Rico; a New York City resident since 1961. Living and traveling in primitive areas made it difficult to pursue an early interest in the harp and composing—so I turned to writing. Learned of haiku in early 1960s and received help and encouragement from Clement Hoyt; haiku published in the haiku magazines and elsewhere, including *Young Students Encyclopedia* (1973). Numerous awards include Orchid Award from *Haiku Magazine*, 1972. Charter member of the Haiku Society of America, president 1971."

Geraldine Clinton Little

"I was born in Portstewart, Ireland, into a family of musicians, artists, and writers. Hold a B.A. degree in English Literature from Goddard College, Plainfield, Vermont, and am currently working on a Master's degree in English. I wrote my first poem of *any* kind in 1968. Became interested in haiku on seeing a copy of Dr. Eric Amann's *Haiku*, and was first published in *Haiku Highlights*. Now publish regularly in all the haiku magazines, and have won a number of awards. Haiku's appeal for me is its 'world in a grain of sand' philosophy, the here and now of it. Other publishing credits include poetry and articles in various magazines (*Bitterroot, New England Review*, etc.) and in four anthologies of the New Jersey Poetry Society, of which I am Chairman of the Leaves of Grass Chapter. I am also a member of the Author's Guild. Have given poetry readings at a number of places, including the Princeton University Library. My first novel is now with an agent."

David Lloyd

"I was born May 9, 1930, in Montclair, New Jersey. At present, I am a professor of English and Communications at Glassboro State College, New Jersey. My haiku, the first of which were published in 1968, have received the following awards: Haiku of the month and year awards from *Haiku Highlights* as well as place prizes in bi-monthly contests; the American Poetry Fellowship award in *Modern Haiku;* award contests in *Dragonfly;* Poet of the Issue award from *Haiku Magazine;* and the R. H. Blyth award from *Haiku West.* My works are regularly published in most of the above as well as *Tweed* in Australia and *Byways* in England. My book, *The Circle: A Collection of Haiku and Inkings,* is forthcoming from Charles E. Tuttle, Co., Inc. of Vermont and Japan. I am a member of the Haiku Society of America, former president of The Leaves of Grass poetry society, former vice president and member of the board of the New Jersey State Poetry Society, and presently do creative writing workshops for the New Jersey State Council of the Arts. For me, haiku is not only a poetic form but also a way of life."

Michael McClintock

"Born in Los Angeles March 31, 1950, to Robert Lloyd and La Dona Valencia.

"English literature and Asian studies, Occidental College, 1968–72. My teachers at Occidental were Robert Ryf, who introduced me to the twentieth century; Marsha Kinder, who introduced me to what a poem is and to what thinking might possibly be, and who co-authored a book called *Close-Up* which has led me to the study of cinema and the application of cinematic principles to linguistic textures, or poems; and Franklyn Josselyn, who pointed to the East and said next to nothing.

"My intentions are primarily to contribute to English poetry a texture not there before, to explore perception in language and advance the uses and values of efficient language, and to enjoy myself.

"Have contributed poems and essays to several magazines, including *California Quarterly* and *South and West*, served on the editorial staffs of *Haiku Highlights* and *Modern Haiku*, and published a collection of poems, *Light Run* (1971)."

Mabelsson Norway

"It was in Massachusetts that I was born to my mother, Marysdaughter Mabel, sixty-two years ago. When I was thirteen she took me with my sister, Mabelsdaughter Nan, to France, where for two years I lived and wandered in their company. Since forsaking home at sixteen, I have dwelt for long periods, not only in Massachusetts, but also in Minnesota, Alabama, Florida, Mexico, Alaska, Colorado, New York, Vermont, Hawaii, Peru, and British Columbia, where I am now to be found. The joys and terrors of my shade-loving life are nature, womanhood, and words. As it takes shape in me, poetry draws its own life directly from the objective logic, from the elementary grammar, of these not unusual passions. Though couched in a language of Europe, my verses derive their form through Japan from China and India; but my poetic voice, with its overtones of Africa and Polynesia, owes the burden of its intimate heraldry to aboriginal America. During these fifteen years of struggle to sort the health from the wealth of the gifted Harold Henderson's critical views, it has only been by bearing all my creative antecedents constantly in mind that I have managed to forge the individuality of my poetic style."

Alan Pizzarelli

"Born 1950 (Capricorn) in Newark, New Jersey.
Poet/Musician.
Learned haiku by reading and writing it
rather than reading and writing about it.
My haiku, senryu, sequences, concrete poems etc
have published in the haiku magazines
and are collected in a book: *Karma Poems*."

Marjory Bates Pratt

"Born 1896 in Waterville, Maine. A.B., Smith College,
1917, Ph.D. (in Psychology), Clark University, 1922. Started
writing haiku after reading J. D. Salinger's 'Seymour: An
Introduction,' published in *The New Yorker* in 1959. The
story referred in a footnote to R. H. Blyth's four-volume
Haiku. Reading Blyth produced an irresistible urge to write
'haiku' in English. Had no idea that others were doing the
same thing, until I heard through Alfred Creager of Ursinus
College about the little magazine *American Haiku*. Began
sending things to it in 1963 and received help and encourage-
ment from the late Clement Hoyt, and from James Bull and
Robert Spiess. Have been published by *American Haiku* and
(after *A.H.* folded in 1968) by *Haiku West*. Was a finalist
in the Japan Air Lines 1964 National Radio Haiku Contest."

Sydell Rosenberg

"I'm a product of New York City and this is very much reflected in my city haiku. Last summer (1972) I received my M.A. in English as a Second Language from Hunter College, and am presently teaching. First published haiku was in 1967. Found haiku to be unphony and demanding. Still do. I write other poetry which gets published, and prose too. Recently had a love poem appear in a marriage anthology published by Abbey Press, *I Love You All Day/It Is That Simple*. Also won third prize in the haiku division of the Poets Tape Exchange, September 1972. I'm now working on a reader for ESL students."

Michael Segers

"Born 10 July 1950 in Macon, Georgia, I have spent most of my life in the South, studying at La Grange College, Georgia Southern College, and the University of Georgia, where I am currently working on my doctorate. I first learned of haiku in a high school English class and have since had the privilege of being influenced by John Wills. I am attempting to create in English a form analogous to and not in imitation of the Japanese haiku."

Ron Seitz

"b. 1935—Louisville, Ky.
poems/prose published thruout U.S./Canada past 5 years,
    about 100 pieces/various places
couple literary awards
Poetry Book published, *Requiem,* 1971 Ghost Press
    Bethlehem Pa.
Empty House Pub. Co. to do 2 poembooks Winter 73/
    Spring 74: *Idiot Sing* & *Bad Meat* (press in Venezuela)
presently Humanities Prof/Bellarmine College/Louisville Ky
also 'published' photographer—a collection soon

Haiku experience:
maybe 15 years writing, but always think that way
poems appear various places time-to-time
an unpublished collection, *Rest Empty* (includes Zen ink
    drawings/'signatures' really)
R. H. Blyth/first intro to Haiku, thanks
little poems/quick-eye snapshot of IT, what/who IS
clean simple poor 'wordless' say to Life
no 'I'/anonymous the poem
silence solitude empty&nothing the poet
Home   Naked   a finger pointing Nowhere"

Robert Spiess

"Have been fifty years a Wisconsinite. I inclined to haiku upon reading Harold Henderson's *The Bamboo Broom* and my first haiku began appearing in 1949 in *American Poetry Magazine*. For several years in the 1960s I was poetry editor of *American Haiku* and in the '70s I have been an associate editor of *Modern Haiku*. The three books of my haiku are *The Heron's Legs* (1966), *The Turtle's Ears* (1971), and *Five Caribbean Haibun* (1972), the first book of original, English language haibun.

"Without expositing on 'form and content,' I prefer to think of the haiku in English as a POEM that, as a norm, has about nine to thirteen simple words esthetically structured in three lines (deriving from the poetically perfected, seventeen-syllable Japanese haiku's division into three parts)—but an English language poem singular in that in using the resources and genius of our language and aspects of our poetics to re-create the haiku moment with words and silence, it also requires the Japanese haiku's disciplined orientation toward heightened awareness, direct perception, immediacy and brevity, suggestion and indirection but nonetheless concreteness and particularization, poetic naturalness . . .

"In my own often 'highly objective' haiku I frequently use multiple-sense imagery (juxtaposition of two or more sense perceptions) to intimate the interrelations within the natural world and between that world and perceiving man (again, no exposition on man as part of the natural world, etc.). Also, I try to make a haiku be a creative unity through, among other associations, a certain calm tension, or else a correspondence, between the thematic elements."

Bonnie Squires

"My high school English teacher Mrs. Margaret Hay introduced me to haiku, and William J. Higginson, editor of *Haiku Magazine*, goaded me into taking haiku seriously. My haiku have appeared in his magazine and in *Modern Haiku*. My free verse has been published in issues of *English Journal*, *Poet*, the journal of the World Poetry Society Intercontinental, and *Moon Age Poets*. At age thirty-three, I reside in a suburb of Philadelphia, am married, and have two children. A former high school English teacher with a Phi Beta Kappa key and M.A. in English from the University of Pennsylvania, I teach a creative writing workshop at the Western Branch of the YMHA, and write a monthly editorial column for the *Jewish Exponent*, an English-language weekly."

Jan S. Streif

"I was born of Clarence & Anne Streif, December 8, 1939, in Alton, Illinois. Began writing haiku in early 1967, interest arriving via the work of Ezra Pound, Harold Henderson's *An Introduction to Haiku*, & *Haiku Highlights* magazine. In 1970, I published a booklet of 44 haiku, *Distant Lanterns*."

Tom Tico

"I was born in San Francisco, May 15, 1942. I live close to the ocean beside Golden Gate Park. I have never cared for school, but have preferred sports and games. Basketball, Frisbee, and Go (five-in-a-row) are present satisfactions. I am married, have two boys and a girl, and work as a mailman.

"In 1966 I happened upon *An Introduction to Haiku* by Harold Henderson. I had been writing haiku (attempts) for a short time. I wrote to him and asked if he would read my haiku and make suggestions. From then on, his generous help and encouragement have been unceasing.

"About the same time, I met James Hackett, whom I consider to be the outstanding haiku poet. He too was exceptionally friendly and encouraging. I often think of the open-heartedness of these two men.

"Originally, certain books drew me to haiku. *The Religions of Man* by Huston Smith was the first, followed by *Walden*, the *Tao Te Ching*, and *Zen Buddhism* by D. T. Suzuki. It was in Suzuki's writings that I first discovered haiku.

"Novels that made a lasting impression and must unconsciously influence my haiku are: *The Keys of the Kingdom* by Cronin, *Siddhartha* by Hesse, and *Zorba the Greek* by Kazantzakis. The poet I esteem above others: Walt Whitman.

"In fields other than literature, Isadora Duncan and Renoir have my highest admiration. And, finally, the greatest influence on my haiku, which somehow encompasses the others: the teachings of Ramakrishna and Vivekananda."

James Tipton

"I raise sheep, teach at Alma College, Michigan, and write. Interested (particularly considering this time of too many words) in the possibility of discovering new energy through words put together with precision and emotion."

Cor van den Heuvel

"Born March 6, 1931, in Biddeford, Maine. First revelations in poetry came in the mid-fifties through the 'thisnesses' of Gerard Manley Hopkins. These and, later, the 'things' of William Carlos Williams have probably had, aside from haiku, the most influence on my work. In 1958 made a pilgrimage to San Francisco's North Beach, where I met briefly some of the poets of the so-called 'renaissance'—and learned a bit of what a long journey I had, and still have, to go to learn this craft. About the same time read Blyth, Henderson, and Yasuda—haiku seemed to hold the key to what I was looking for in poetry. They were able to create, with more depth and immediacy than I'd ever found before, that miracle of incarnation where words become an ontological presence offering a glimpse of the infinite.

"Began writing haiku early 1959 in Wells Beach, Maine, and read them and translations of Japanese haiku in the Café Zen in Ogunquit that summer. Gave readings of haiku and other poetry regularly for a while in coffee houses in Boston. In winter of '60–'61 became involved for a short time in the 'East Side Scene' at the Tenth Street Coffee House in New York City, and began printing my haiku on a small hand-press. For several years I continued to write & print my books unaware of the growing number of other poets writing haiku. Discovered the Haiku Society and the world of haiku magazines winter '71–'72.

"Education: B.A. English Literature 1957, University of New Hampshire; M.A. English Literature 1968, New York University. Magazines & other media: Poems have appeared in *Haiku Magazine* and *Haiku West;* have read my work on radio stations in Boston and New York, and on TV in New Hampshire. Books: *sun in skull* (1961), *a bag of marbles* (1962), *the window-washer's pail* (1963), *EO7* (1964), *BaNG* (1966), *water in a stone depression* (1969), all published by Chant Press, New York."

Anita Virgil

"My acquaintance with haiku came accidentally. A three-line poem published by *Haiku Highlights* in 1968 (submitted to them simply because they accepted poems of eight lines or under) drew comment from William J. Higginson. A correspondence resulted from this which led me to the works of R. H. Blyth, Harold G. Henderson, and to Eric Amann of Toronto, then editor of *Haiku Magazine*. What I learned from these four individuals coincided with much of what I had been aware of in my studies of art. I saw the haiku as a logical extension of all I had known and preferred: drawing that is spare and essential, the particular and the whole implied by it, Nature in its broadest sense—the nature of all things of this world: their unique identity and yet their sameness, their evanescence and their eternal quality. I feel no less at home with a Rembrandt drawing than with an assemblage by Rauschenberg, no further from haiku watching a TV documentary on the Ngorogoro Plain than I am when savoring Buson's anticipation of Vuillard in his eighteenth-century scroll 'The Elysium of the Peach Blossom Spring.' The centuries telescope because of artists: what is fresh and vigorous is always so.

"Born in Baltimore, Maryland. Now resident of Montclair, New Jersey. Formal educational training in art (though always involved with literature). Graduate of High School of Music and Art, New York City; art courses at Art Students League, NYU, CCNY. Worked as editorial assistant in the Art Department of *Town & Country* magazine. In 1972, invited to give one-woman show of eighty mushroom paintings at the New York Horticultural Society. Poems, reviews, essays have appeared in haiku magazines in the United States, England, and Japan. Became President of the Haiku Society of America in 1973."

Nicholas Virgilio

"I was born in Camden, New Jersey, June 28, 1928, under a full moon. After graduating from Camden High School, I enlisted in the Navy (1946–48). Following the service, I went to the College of South Jersey and Temple University, getting a B.A. in Radio Broadcasting in 1952.

"I worked on radio stations in different parts of the country for several years, returning to Camden in 1958. In Dallas, Texas, in 1957, the end of a love affair resulted in a strange, religious experience. For three days I was supremely sane—and could see all the insanity around me as clearly as in a Goya painting. It was then that I began to write poetry.

"In 1962 I discovered haiku through Kenneth Yasuda's book, *A Pepper Pod*. My first haiku was published the following year by *American Haiku*, and I am deeply indebted to the editors of that magazine, especially James Bull and Clement Hoyt, for encouraging my early efforts.

"I began giving readings of my poetry at schools, colleges, and to community groups in 1967, and have spoken, among many other places, at Cornell, the University of Pennsylvania, Temple, Villanova, the University of Virginia, and Rutgers. I have also read my work on a number of radio and TV stations in Philadelphia, and co-directed the First International Haiku Festival at the University of Pennsylvania in May 1971.

"When not away giving lectures and readings of haiku, I write and study in my home at 1092 Niagara Road in Camden, or wander along the branches of nearby Newton Creek where I get some of my best haiku.

"The encouragement and advice of Harold G. Henderson and Leroy Kanterman, editor of *Haiku West*, have been of great help to me. My work is quoted and discussed in Henderson's *Haiku in English*, and has appeared in numerous magazines and newspapers.

"Without the support and faith of my parents, my poems might never have been written."

Gerald Robert Vizenor

"Born in Minneapolis, Minnesota, in 1934. As a young man lived in Japan for two years, where I wrote my first haiku from personal experiences. Studied oriental literature at the University of Minnesota, and attended New York University and Harvard University. Have published five books of haiku.

"The elusive energy of haiku—that probity of perception and experience—is found everywhere in literature. For me the concise images of haiku are special moments of life from the fragments of memory and visual experience. Haiku is a way of knowing the fragile movements of the world."

Books: *Two Wings the Butterfly*, 1962, printed privately; *Raising the Moon Vines*, 1964, *Seventeen Chirps*, 1964, *Slight Abrasions: A Dialogue with Jerome Downes*, 1966, and *Empty Swings*, 1967, all published by Nodin Press, Minneapolis.

Larry Wiggin

"Born in Northfield, New Hampshire, November 15, 1919 . . . usual schooling . . . served in the Army during World War Two, in the South Pacific . . . taught elementary school for four years . . . operated a dairy farm for thirteen years . . . am a certified Swedish Masseur, practicing since 1963 . . . am presently employed at the Lakes Region General Hospital, in Laconia, New Hampshire.

"Interest in brevity started with the short stories of Hemingway . . . interest in haiku began with a Peter Pauper Press edition of *The Four Seasons*, a collection of Japanese haiku . . . dislike detail in writing, save a necessary scientific explanation of how something works, or how to open and cook a package of frozen peas . . . believe the majority of poets get carried away with their own rhetoric and what they have to say could be said in half the space . . . Bible is an excellent example of compression of expression.

"Since 1961, have written only haiku, trying over the years to break from the classical Japanese tradition of a seventeen-syllable count and the 'season word,' to make the haiku an American idiom.

"Have been published in *Haiku Magazine, Haiku Highlights, Haiku West, Dragonfly, Yankee Magazine*, and in a number of newspapers . . . edited *Variations of Mulberry*, an anthology of haiku, published by the Poetry Society of New Hampshire.

"Note: was asked to write this sketch in first person, and so I have, leaving the 'I' understood. Hate the damn word, personally!"

Rod Willmot

"Prior to 1948 I think I was a hermit thrush somewhere in Algonquin; when reincarnated in Toronto as a human being I felt distinctly out of place. I was born with several incurable diseases—writing in my bones, music in my blood, and an inability to sit still. Spent my youth biting the dust all across Canada. I discovered haiku when a friend edited one of my poems down to the last three lines; since then I've always had the highest regard for brevity and illiterate friends. However, when my book *Haiku* (1969) was published, I decided to write novels instead."

John Wills

Born on July 4, 1921, in Los Angeles.

"Have been teaching English and American literature for over twenty years in colleges and universities throughout the eastern United States. M.A. from the University of Chicago, Ph.D. from Washington University in St. Louis. For many years focused upon literary criticism, publishing articles in academic journals on T. S. Eliot, Conrad, and Walter de la Mare. In 1968 turned to haiku, and with the encouragement of Eric Amann, Rhoda Jewell, Anita Virgil, and William J. Higginson began to put out my books—*Weathervanes* (1969), *Back Country* (1969), *river* (1970), *The Young Leaves* (1970), and *Cornstubble* (1971).

"During the summer of 1970, with a faculty research grant from Georgia Southern College, wrote and studied haiku in Matsuyama, Japan. Have for many years—in Minnesota, Wisconsin, North Carolina, Georgia—preferred living outside town, up the least-travelled roads, in the back country of my haiku. Now live on (and poetically exploit) a hundred acres of land in the mountains of Tennessee, where I am working on my sixth volume of haiku, *mountain*. My wife, Marlene, with her closeup nature photography and haiga-like ink sketches, has collaborated with me on my last four books—the last three of which are still available in limited quantities (for information write the Haiku Society of America)."

Kenneth Yasuda

One of the most important writers in English on the Japanese haiku, Kenneth Yasuda also has the distinction of being one of the earliest, possibly the first, to write English language haiku. An American of Japanese descent, he was born in Auburn, California, on June 23, 1914. After graduating from the University of Washington in 1938, he studied in Japan until 1941. On his return to the United States, he began work on *A Pepper Pod* (published in 1947), an anthology of Japanese haiku translated into English together with a selection of his own original English language haiku. In 1944, because of his Japanese origin, he was sent to relocation centers in Arkansas and Wyoming. After the war he did graduate work at Columbia University. He then returned to Japan and worked as a court interpreter and textbook specialist for the U.S. Department of State, 1946–49. From 1951 to 1960 he worked in Tokyo for the Asia Foundation, and in 1956 received the degree of Doctor of Literature in Japanese from the University of Tokyo—the first American to receive that honor. Dr. Yasuda taught at the University of Hawaii from 1960–67, and since then has been a professor at Indiana University. He has published the following books: *A Pepper Pod*, Alfred A. Knopf, New York, 1947; an English translation of the *Minase Sangin Hyakuin,* Kogakusha, Tokyo, 1956; *The Japanese Haiku,* Charles E. Tuttle Co., Rutland, Vermont, and Tokyo, 1957; *Land of the Reed Plains: Ancient Japanese Lyrics from the Manyoshu,* Charles E. Tuttle Co., 1961; and *Six Noh Plays,* Kofusha, Tokyo, 1967–68.

In a letter to the editor dated April 2, 1973, Dr. Yasuda had the following to say about his early experiences with haiku:

"To answer some of the questions you raise, I began writing haiku in both English and Japanese in high school. Clark Ashton Smith, the very fine poet and short story writer, who in his early days was in touch with the Jack London group in California, was a near and dear neighbor, who shared his sensitivity and joy with me. We wrote haiku for each other. He had a very fine ear. . . . During the late 1930s, when I

277

was a student at the University of California, the student paper ran my haiku quite frequently and I also used to contribute to the Japanese language papers on the west coast in Japanese. After the war began John Gould Fletcher would visit the war relocation camp in Arkansas, and in his letters would include haiku as a postscript. . . . In the camps there was always a group of Japanese who came together to write haiku for each other. I recollect once as a very young student writing to Kyoshi Takahama, the modern haiku master, and he published my enthusiastic letter in his magazine in Japan—it must have bemused him in those pre-World War II days to get such a letter from America. I also knew Miyamori and through him met Takahama later, in 1938 or 1939. Such were my haiku roots."

Virginia Brady Young

"I was born in New York City and attended Columbia University but did not have the finances to obtain a degree. I have published three books of poetry, *The Clooney Beads* and *Double Windows* by Folder Editions, New York, and *Circle of Thaw* by Barlenmir House, New York. In 1974 Barlenmir will bring out another collection of my poems entitled *Dark Balloons.* I have studied with Robert Frost, Philip Booth, and Anne Sexton and, at the request of William Stafford who was Poetry Consultant of the Library of Congress, recorded my poems for the permanent poetry collection of the library. At present I am Vice President of the Haiku Society of America.

"My early interest in haiku came from reading the first haiku magazine published in the United States—*American Haiku.* Later, during a trip to Japan, I became deeply absorbed in the shape and texture of rocks, the nuances of water, the shapes of trees. After Japan I wrote a different kind of haiku, closer to nature because I was closer to nature. Over the years I have found the art of haiku demanding, at times overwhelming, and more satisfactory for catching the spontaneous and intuitive flashes which can so easily escape the poet."